HOW TO REACH THE WEST AGAIN

BY TIMOTHY KELLER

REDEEMER
CITY to CITY

Print ISBN: 9780578633756
Ebook ISBN: 9780578642437

HOW TO REACH THE WEST AGAIN

BY TIMOTHY KELLER

For 30 years, we've been told that Western society is becoming post-Christian and that the church must adapt to a changing culture in order to remain relevant. Despite this gloomy prediction, Christianity has displayed remarkable staying power. There are parts of North America where substantial numbers of people still hold traditional religious and moral beliefs. While mainline churches have declined, evangelical churches largely have not.[1] It might be more accurate to say that instead of being thoroughly post-Christian, America today is still marked by "spotty Christendom" in many places.

But the overall decline of Christian influence in the West is inarguable. Each generation is becoming less religious and less Christian. More than two-thirds of the churches in the United States have plateaued or are in decline.[2] While religion was broadly seen as a social good, or at least benign, increasing numbers of people now see the church as bad for people and a major obstacle to social progress. Traditional Christian beliefs about sexuality and gender are being viewed as dangerous and restrictive of people's basic civil rights.

Instead of wringing our hands over the loss of cultural influence in Western culture, this decline should prompt us to examine ourselves, pray, and work toward a new missionary engagement with Western culture. We have to model and proclaim the Christian faith in our generation in a way that is both intelligible and compelling to our neighbors.

The main challenges to having this sort of encounter have been the same over the centuries. One is spiritual

---

[1] "In U.S., Decline of Christianity Continues at Rapid Pace," Pew Research Center's Religion & Public Life Project, November 12, 2019. https://www.pewforum.org/2019/10/17/in-u-s-decline-of-christianity-continues-at-rapid-pace/ See also https://religioninpublic.blog/2019/10/24/american-religion-in-2030/

[2] "Small, Struggling Congregations Fill U.S. Church Landscape," *LifeWay Research*, Marvch 6, 2019. https://lifewayresearch.com/2019/03/06/small-struggling-congregations-fill-u-s-church-landscape

pride. Jonathan Edwards reflected on how revivals were often undermined by human pride, which can manifest itself in unnecessary disunity, fractiousness, and tribalism among Christians.[3] Another abiding challenge is syncretism—when believers mix their faith with the idols of the culture, as in the book of Judges (Judges 2:11-15). While we may not be tempted toward literal polytheism, Christians in the West today certainly have to resist the lure of cultural idols, especially those that promise political power or social relevance.

Today's culture believes the thing we need salvation from is the idea that we need salvation.

Along with commonalities, each age has its own unique challenges. Today, churches in Western society have to deal with something they have never faced before—a culture increasingly hostile to their faith that is not merely non-Christian (such as in China, India, and Middle Eastern countries), but post-Christian. What are the biggest obstacles we are facing in our cultural moment?

---

[3] Jonathan Edwards, *The Works of Jonathan Edwards. Vol. 1* (Edinburgh: Banner of Truth Trust, 1995), 397-403.

THE CHALLENGE OF EVANGELISM IN A POST-CHRISTIAN WORLD

For centuries, Christians have been able to assume that everyone around them believed in a "sacred order"—a transcendent, supernatural dimension of reality that was the ground of moral absolutes and promised life after death. All cultures believed in a standard of right and wrong to which human beings were obligated to conform regardless of their feelings. They therefore also believed in objective guilt and sin, and that the problems of human life are solved when we connect to that sacred order rather than simply live for ourselves. Of course, Muslims, Hindus, Buddhists, and animists disagreed (even violently) over *what* that sacred order was and rejected the Christian account of it, but everyone agreed that it existed and we needed to find a way to touch it.

Late modern culture is the first culture based on a rejection of a "sacred order." In the name of individual freedom, today's society declares that there are no transcendent realities to which we must conform. Rather, we choose our own values and create our own meaning in life. Academic, artistic, and entertainment institutions teach that the only "sacred" depths are the ones found within us. Indeed, if there is a moral absolute in today's culture, it is that we must *not* say that there are moral absolutes, let alone a sacred order with which all people must align. Such statements are said to oppress people and limit their freedom.

Past evangelistic strategies assumed that nearly everyone held this shared set of beliefs about a sacred order—that there was a God, an afterlife, a standard of moral truth, and a sense of sin. We might call these the "religious dots" that evangelists could assume in their hearers. Evangelism was simply connecting the dots that listeners already possessed in order to prove the truth of the gospel. Today's culture believes the thing we need salvation from is the idea that we need salvation.

How, then, do you evangelize people who lack any sense of sin or transcendence, or who lack the traditional basic religious infrastructure such as belief in a Supreme Being or the afterlife? The church in the West has not faced this situation before.

THE CHALLENGE OF FORMING CHRISTIAN DISCIPLES IN A DIGITAL CULTURE

In the United States, the average person now spends two and a half hours a day on social media.[4] In 2015, the average 12th grader was online for four hours a day; younger people spend much more time and are

7

more profoundly shaped by the internet.[5] In *Reclaiming Conversation*, Sherry Turkle of MIT says that increased time on social media correlates with a measurable loss of empathy—the ability to put ourselves in someone else's shoes.[6] More and more, what is outside seems less real than what is inside one's head and feelings. That means:

- Technology conveys the narratives and beliefs of secular modernity regarding identity, freedom, happiness, and relativism in an immersive way, far beyond what TV, radio, or movies could ever do.

- Technology doesn't merely give us different beliefs. It changes the very way we form them. Beliefs become very thin, chosen only if they fit how we want to see ourselves and easily discarded when they do not.

---

[4] "Average Time Spent Daily on Social Media (with 2019 Data)," *BroadbandSearch*. Accessed October 1, 2019. https://www.broadbandsearch.net/blog/average-daily-time-on-social-media#post-navigation-1

[5] "Teens Today Spend More Time on Digital Media, Less Time Reading," *American Psychological* Association. Accessed October 1, 2019. https://www.apa.org/news/press/releases/2018/08/teenagers-read-book

[6] Sherry Turkle, *Reclaiming Conversation: The Power of Talk in a Digital Age* (New York: Penguin, 2015).

The challenges of formation in such a digital culture are considerable. Our traditional models of biblical and spiritual formation through just a few hours of public worship time and a community group are insufficient for countering the impact of 24/7 digital technology throughout the week. Our models of theological formation give us a firm grasp of biblical doctrine, which is indispensable, but they fail to deconstruct culture's beliefs and provide better, Christian answers to the questions of the late modern human heart.

This is one of the bitter fruits of the secular project, the first effort in history to build cohesive societies without a common set of shared moral and religious values.

THE CHALLENGE OF POLITICAL POLARIZATION IN A FRAGMENTED CULTURE

Across the West and elsewhere, we are experiencing increasing amounts of political polarization.[7] There is

7 Thomas Carothers and Andrew O'Donohue. "How to Understand the Global Spread of Political Polarization," Carnegie Endowment for International Peace. Accessed November 21, 2019. https://carnegieendowment.org/2019/10/01/how-to-understand-global-spread-of-political-polarization-pub-79893

enormous dissatisfaction with the political establishment, and people are willing to vote for candidates, both right and left, who would have been considered extreme just ten years ago. This is one of the bitter fruits of the secular project, the first effort in history to build cohesive societies without a common set of shared moral and religious values.

James Eglinton describes the two poles of our fragmented culture in an article for *Christianity Today* entitled "Populism vs Progressivism: Who Knows Best?" He identifies, "the emergence of two rival visions of the world…"

> One attracts those receptive to the restoration of national greatness, the importance of groups over individuals, and the conservation of the past. The other pulls on those receptive to a starkly individualistic future, unhitched from the obligations of the past, and bound, instead, to the notion of progress. Crucially, each of these cultural forces also repels those who prove unreceptive to it. For this reason, our cultural commentators now talk of "Two Americas," "Two Brazils," and "Two United Kingdoms."

> In each of these settings, populations migrate toward opposite polar extremities…[8]

One of these views makes an idol out of individual freedom, the other out of race and nation, blood and soil. Both are secular—the transcendent God is missing, and something created and earthly is deified.

The great danger is churches getting caught up in this polarization and becoming mere tools of either a leftward or rightward political coalition. In America, for example, the country is now seeing the development of both "blue evangelicalism" and "red evangelicalism." The former talks about racial and economic justice, but is quiet about the biblical teaching on subjects such as sexuality, gender, and family. The latter condemns sexual immorality and secularism, but grows silent when its political allies fan the flames of racial resentment toward immigrants and minority communities. When the church, in the interests of acquiring political power, aligns too much with the current age's secular left or right, it is sapped of both spiritual power and credibility with non-Christians. We see "the political captivity of the faithful."[9]

---

[8] James Eglinton, "Populism vs. Progressivism: Who Knows Best?" *Christianity Today*. November 20, 2018. Accessed August 21, 2019. https://www.christianitytoday.com/ct/2018/november-web-only/politics-polarization-populism-vs-progressivism-who-knows-b.html

[9] See Dr. Nathan O. Hatch's "The Political Captivity of the Faithful" at https://rap.wustl.edu/video/the-political-captivity-of-the-faithful/

The solution cannot be some imaginary apolitical withdrawal (as if that were possible). Christians must learn to do something new—to engage politically, yet critically, not capitulating to any reigning ideology, in order to truly be "salt and light" in society rather than part of its decay.

THE ELEMENTS OF A MISSIONARY ENCOUNTER

These three challenges must be tackled directly and deliberately. Christian leaders must dedicate time and talent to developing strategies that will overcome these barriers to a gospel movement in our generation.

We are entering a new era in which, in many places in the West, there is not only no social benefit to being a Christian, but an actual social cost to espousing faith. Culture is becoming more actively hostile toward Christian beliefs and practices. Semi-biblical, generically religious beliefs in God, truth, sin, and the afterlife (the "religious dots") are disappearing in more and more people as culture produces people for whom Christianity is not only offensive, but incomprehensible. Therefore, we must find ways of evangelizing people who lack the "religious dots" and would never think of coming to church. And we must find ways of churching and forming people as Christians in the midst of a very different culture.

To clarify, a missionary encounter is *not* a withdrawal from culture into communities with little connection to the rest of society. Nor is it an effort to secure political power in order to impose Christian standards and beliefs on an unwilling populace. Nor is it an effort to become so "relevant" that the church becomes completely adapted to and assimilated into the culture.

Instead, a missionary encounter *connects* (unlike the strategies of withdrawal), yet *confronts* (unlike the strategies of assimilation), and therefore actually *converts* people (unlike all the strategies, including those of political domination). And while critiquing all the other strategies at a fundamental level, a church embarked on a missionary encounter *does* maintain its distinctiveness (a goal shared with the withdrawal approach). It *does* often affirm and always serve its neighbors (a goal shared with the assimilation approach). It *does* call people to repent and change (a goal occasionally shared with the politically assertive approach).

In many ways, we must look to the early church that had an effective missionary encounter with a very hostile culture. And yet, since our Western culture is *post*-Christian and the challenges it poses are unique, our generation's missionary encounter will not look exactly like any missionary encounter that the church has had in the past.[10]

There are six basic elements to having a missionary encounter with Western culture.[11]

CHRISTIAN HIGH THEORY

Before we can explain the gospel to a culture, we must analyze that culture with the gospel.

Over the last couple of centuries, the subject of apologetics has involved giving arguments and evidences for the truth of Christianity, such as stating a case for the historicity of the Resurrection. This approach goes back to the New Testament (1 Corinthians 15). But the early Christian apologists, from Justin Martyr to Augustine, did more than that. They did not merely try to show that Christian practice and belief were just as rational as the dominant pagan culture. They developed a radical critique of the dominant culture that showed how it failed to measure up to its own standards. After the sack of

---

[10] As I will explain in more detail later on, these three wrong approaches to culture (above called domination, assimilation, and withdrawal) follow James D. Hunter who calls them "Defensive Against," "Relevant To," and "Purity From." His alternative is "faithful presence within"—Christians are not to withdraw but be fully present in the public realms, yet faithfully and unashamedly identifying as believers, all with a servant stance that seeks the common good. See James D. Hunter, *To Change the World: The Irony, Tragedy, and Possibility of Christianity in the Late Modern World* (Oxford, 2010).

[11] See: Larry Hurtado, *Destroyer of the Gods* (Baylor, 2017). Also see point #5 below, "Faithful Christian Presence in Public Spheres."

Rome in 410, for example, pagan Romans were quick to blame the destruction on the Christians. By their reckoning, the Roman gods let their city fall as punishment for worshipping this new Christian God. This claim led Augustine to write *The City of God*, in which he developed what today would be called "critical theory," or high theory. He used the gospel to critique the foundations of pagan culture as inconsistent with its own aspirations. Further, he argued that paganism itself—not Christianity—was to blame for the destruction of Rome.

Today, a Christian high theory might profitably begin by questioning our culture's claims to neutrality, objectivity, and universality. It would engage the late modern secular view of the world publicly. It should show how, in an effort to free the individual self, culture has led to our current condition in which:

- All values are relative,

- All relationships are transactional,

- All identities are fragile, and

- All (supposed) sources of fulfillment are disappointing.

And so, ironically, we are still not *free*: not free objectively, as local communities and families decline, as public and private bureaucracies—impenetrable and unresponsive—dominate our lives; and not free subjectively, as we experience inner loneliness and enslaving addictions.

Christian theory must be able to escape political captivity. It can do that by using the biblical doctrine of God and gospel to critique the forms of secular modernity that reduce human life to purely individual choices or reduce it to the product of historical, material, and social forces (leading to both libertarian conservatism and progressive Marxism, respectively). Christian high theory must first expose the main flaws in our culture's narratives, showing how they fit neither human nature nor our most profound intuitions about life—let alone its own moral ideals. Then, Christian theory must point to the beauty and truth of the gospel as the fulfilling counter-narrative.

This work is largely going to be that of Christians in the academy and the help of non-Christian scholars and thinkers who have also seen the fatal flaws in late modernity. Many of these people have already focused on the problem of unchecked individualism, the problem of the late modern self, and the problem of relativism—all of which are intensified in today's late modern culture.[12]

A TRULY POST-CHRISTENDOM EVANGELISTIC DYNAMIC

Western churches have many evangelistic methods and programs but, as we saw above, they all assumed that there were still non-Christians in society who would seek out the church (or at least be open to an invitation to come), who held basic concepts of God, truth, sin, and an afterlife, and who thought that, even if they did not believe, religion was a positive good for many people. For 1,000 years, the Western church's basic ministry model was premised on the social reality that people would be *coming, prepared, and positive,* and we could simply preach our sound biblical sermons to them. Increasingly, this is not the case. If it is true that more and more people lack any religious foundation and that the dominant cultural narratives are making the Christian faith more offensive, then we must find new and compelling ways to share the gospel in this generation. In fact, we must discover a late modern version of the evangelistic dynamic of the early

12 The following resources have been formative for my thinking on these issues: Charles Taylor, *Sources of the Self: The Making of the Modern Identity* (Harvard University Press, 1989) and *A Secular Age* (Harvard University Press, 2007); Robert Bellah, *Habits of the Heart: Individualism and Commitment in American Life* (University of California Press, 1985); Philip Rieff, *The Triumph of the Therapeutic: Uses of Faith After Freud* (Intercollegiate Studies Institute, 1966); and Alasdair MacIntyre, *After Virtue: A Study in Moral Theory* (University of Notre Dame Press, 1981). Bob Goudzwaard and Craig G. Bartholomew offer a helpful summary of many of these issues from a Christian perspective in *Beyond the Modern Age: An Archaeology of Contemporary Culture* (InterVarsity Press, 2017).

church, which grew through conversion in a similarly hostile and uncomprehending culture. The elements of such a dynamic include:

Attention

How do we get people to pay attention to the gospel when they find it irrelevant?

Michael Green estimates that 80% or more of evangelism in the early church was done not by ministers or evangelists, but by ordinary Christians explaining themselves to their *oikos*—their network of relatives and close associates.[13] People paid attention to the gospel because someone they knew well, worked with, and perhaps loved, spoke to them about it.

The greatest challenge today is to stimulate a significantly sized percentage of Christians to intentionally adopt "missional living" in their daily lives and relationships.[14] As Alan Noble notes in *Disruptive Witness*, late modern people are more open to considering Christianity when reading or watching stories and narratives that witness to Christian insights, and during times of stress,

---

[13] Michael Green, *Evangelism in the Early Church* (Eerdmans, 2004).

[14] *Spiritual Conversations in the Digital Age: How Christians Approach to Sharing Their Faith Has Changed in 25 Years* (Barna Group, 2018).

The late modern view of reality and the self does not fit human nature as God designed it. There are times in which stories and art reveal how today's beliefs pinch and fail to satisfy.

difficulty, disappointment, or suffering.[15] Why?

All worldviews that are not biblically based are like a suit of clothes that are too small. Such clothes always uncomfortably pinch—and occasionally they actually rip. The late modern view of reality and the self does not fit human nature as God designed it. There are times in which stories and art reveal how today's beliefs pinch and fail to satisfy. There are other times—especially times of pain—that the late modern worldview "rips" and wholly fails to provide what is needed to face such experiences. Christians need to be prepared in these moments to "give an answer to everyone who asks [them] to give the reason for the hope that [they] have" (1 Peter 3:15).

This entire project assumes Christians will know enough about the Bible and their faith to engage in conversations with others. But it also assumes believers have many relationships with non-Christians, that the average Christian is in close proximity to non-Christians. When

---

15 Alan Noble, *Disruptive Witness: Speaking Truth in a Distracted Age* (InterVarsity Press, 2018).

that isn't the case, the first and most important step is to focus on building personal relationships with non-Christians by befriending and loving them, since they are increasingly unlikely to go to church on their own.

Attraction

Helping non-Christians recognize they have a problem that requires salvation will mean *questioning people's answers* even before the more traditional apologetic method of *answering people's questions* or objections about Christianity. By "people's answers," we mean the working answers to the big questions of life that everyone must have. No one can live without meaning, satisfaction, freedom, identity, forgiveness (given and received), resolution of moral questions, and hope for the future. The culture's ways to provide these things ultimately will not work (they will at least "pinch" and sometimes "rip"). If we have people's attention we can, at the opportune time, point to the unsurpassed resources of Christianity for each:

- A meaning in life that suffering can't take away, but can even deepen

- A satisfaction that isn't based on circumstances

- A freedom that doesn't reduce community and relationships to thin transactions

- An identity that isn't fragile or based on our performance or the exclusion of others

- A way to both deal with guilt and forgive others without residual bitterness or shame

- A basis for seeking justice that does not turn us into oppressors ourselves

- A way to face not only the future, but death itself with poise and peace

- An explanation for the senses of transcendent beauty and love we often experience

Put another way, we must help non-Christians see that their indelible needs and longings for these things are actually echoes of their need for God.

Demonstration

There is a definite need to address the traditional objections to Christian faith—we must still "answer people's questions." These objections cluster around God ("How can a good God allow suffering?" or "How can God send people to hell?") and around the Bible (its historical reliability or compatibility with science). But today, non-Christians ask questions especially about the church's historical record of injustice in regards to slavery, the oppression of women, and the exclusion of gay and trans persons. These issues must be faced with a combination of humility and clarity, and also with a gentle insistence that doubters recognize the assumptions and moral judgments on which their objections rest, which themselves are leaps of faith.

Conviction

We also have to explain the gospel in a way that is compelling and attracts late modern people. The gospel is that "Salvation comes from the Lord" (Jonah 2:9). Gospel presentations must always make two points:

- **The bad news:** You are trying to save yourself, but you can't.

- **The good news:** You can be saved through Christ alone, not your efforts.

In traditional culture, in which the basic narrative is "the meaning of life is to be good," the bad news and good news look like this:

- **The bad news:** You know you should be good, but you aren't good enough in your behavior, nor truly good at all when you look at motives of your heart (e.g., though you don't commit adultery, you have lust in your heart (Matthew 5:27-8)).

• **The good news:** Jesus has taken the punishment your moral failures deserve, so you can be permanently forgiven (e.g., now there is no condemnation for those in Christ Jesus (Romans 8:1)).

In late modern culture, in which the basic narrative is "the meaning of life is to be free," the bad and good news may look like this:

• **The bad news:**

  • You want to be free, but you are not. You must live for something, and whatever it is will enslave you and lead you to exploit others.

  • The existential justification/identity you seek is impossibly fragile and will lead you to exclude others.

  • The deep satisfaction you seek is elusive and can't be found in this world.

  • The explanation for all of this is that you were created by the true God. Your failure to live for him is a violation of both obligation and love.

- **The good news:**

  - On the cross, Jesus reversed the power dynamics of the world, giving up power in service rather than exploiting, and took the just penalty for our unjust rejection of God and treatment of others.

  - This provides an identity unlike any other, one that provides unconditional love and is not based on the ups and downs of our performance.

  - This identity creates a new freedom from being controlled by any force or object in the world, and also provides a foretaste and assured promise of deep satisfaction and beauty in the future.

These elements of evangelism—attention, attraction, demonstration, conviction—will each need to be rethought in our time. "Attention" and "attraction" will largely be accomplished by Christians in their personal relationships, which we have said means that Christians must have deep relationships with non-Christians (and this must be done in a culture in which all face-to-face relationships are thinning out). Christian leaders need to equip laypeople with the tools and resources to have evangelistic and apologetic conversations. If these relationships are established, churches will then need to provide a great variety of venues in which people considering the faith can be helped through the stages of "attraction," "demonstration," and "conviction." This can be done through talks, teaching and preaching, through dialogues and conversations, through small groups and large gatherings, through worship, stories, and art.

A CATEGORY-DEFYING SOCIAL VISION

In *Destroyer of the Gods*, Larry Hurtado seeks to explain why an increasing number of people converted to Christianity in the Roman world, even though it was the most persecuted of all religions and carried significant social cost. Hurtado suggests that part of the answer was the Christian social project—a unique kind of human community that defied categories then and still does today.[16] It has at least five elements that can be broken down and expounded at greater length, but which also need to be seen together, as they constitute a whole. The early church's social vision was:

Multi-racial and multi-ethnic

The Christian religious identity was shocking to the pagans. Previously, you were born into your religion.

---

[16] Larry Hurtado, *Destroyer of the Gods* (Baylor, 2017).

Each race, country, and location had its own gods, and therefore no one ever chose their gods or their religion. Rather, you simply inherited the religion that was essentially an extension of your culture. That meant that all the people who shared your religion were culturally homogeneous—your race determined your faith. It also meant that your race and culture received divine sanction and could never be critiqued.

But Christians believed that there was one true God and everyone should put their faith in him. That meant your faith was not only independent of your race—it was more fundamental. It gave you a bond with all other Christians that was deeper than any other. When a person of any race or culture put their faith in Christ, it gave them a new perspective on their inherited culture and a new multi-racial, multi-ethnic community, the first one formed by any religion.

(See Acts 13:1-3 and Ephesians 2:11-22.)

Highly committed to caring for the poor and marginalized

In that time period, it was considered normal to care for the poor and needy of one's family and tribe, but no one felt obligated to care for *all* poor and needy people, especially not barbarians. But based on Jesus'

Good Samaritan parable (Luke 10:25-37), the early church shockingly embraced all who were in need. The pagan emperor Julian famously remarked that the radical Christian practice of "caring not only for their own poor, but for ours as well" was both offensive and attractive.[17]

(See Galatians 6:10 and Luke 10:25-37.)

Non-retaliatory, marked by a commitment to forgiveness

The early Christians were notable in that, if you attacked or killed them, they did not organize retaliation or get revenge. They were famous for experiencing death in arenas or by execution as they prayed for their persecutors (following the examples of Stephen and Jesus himself). The Christian teaching on forgiveness and "turning the other cheek" created a community of peace-making, reconciliation, and bridge-building.

(See Romans 12:14-21 and 1 Peter 2:11-12, 21-23.)

Strongly and practically against abortion and infanticide

Christians were dead-set against both abortion and infanticide, but not merely in principle. They found and

---

[17] *The Works of the Emperor Julian*, Vol. III (Loeb Classical Library, 1913).

took in infants who were thrown out to die or become harvested by slavers. The early church was "pro-life," especially in the sense that they recognized no gradations of human value. In a tribalized, socially-stratified shame-and-honor culture, that was shocking.

(See Luke 1:15, James 1:27, and Psalm 139:13-16.)

Revolutionizing the sex ethic

In the Roman world, sex was merely an appetite. Its purpose was to serve the social order. Married women could not have sex with anyone but their husbands. But men—even married ones—could have sex with any male or female they wanted, as long as it was with someone of less honor and class. Christianity's revolutionary teaching detached sex and marriage from the social order and connected it to the cosmic—to God's saving love and redemption. God gave himself to us by going to the cross, and we must respond by giving ourselves utterly and exclusively to him and no other god. This saving love brought about an astonishing union between two radically different beings—God and humanity.

Therefore, sex was not for self-gratification, but for giving one's whole life in a consensual marriage covenant that fostered deep unity across the difference of male and female and combined their non-reproducible excellencies. This was a high, attractive vision of the character of sex, and it took enormous power away from men and the upper classes. Christianity was immensely attractive to women, who saw it as an equalizing and empowering religion.

(See 1 Corinthians 6:12-7:5.)

The early Christian community was both offensive and attractive. But believers did not construct this community as a way to reach Roman culture. Rather, each of the five elements listed above characterized the early church because Christians sought to submit to biblical authority. They are all commands as well as implications of the gospel.

These five elements are just as category-defying, just as offensive and attractive, today. The first two views on ethnic diversity and caring for the poor sound "liberal" and the last two views on abortion and sexual ethics sound "conservative." The third element, being non-retaliatory, sounds like no particular party today, and is commonly rejected in today's culture of outrage. Churches today are under enormous pressure to jettison the first two or the last two, but not to keep them all. Yet to give up any of them would make Christianity the handmaid of a particular political program and undermine the missionary encounter.

To model the spirit of the early church, the late modern Christian social vision today should include:

Building a multi-ethnic church

Not every community is multi-ethnic, and so not every church can or should be multi-ethnic. But, in general, it is both theologically warranted (Ephesians 2) and missionally effective in our culture for North American churches to be as multi-ethnic as possible and to learn from and be connected to the multi-racial global church. In a world divided by tribe and race, there is no greater witness to the power of the gospel. Richard Bauckham has pointed out that the Christian church is the most globally-distributed religion.[18] It shows greater cultural flexibility than any other religion. The reasons include the very concept of salvation by grace and the fact that the New Testament has no book of Leviticus filled with prescriptions for a particular cultural pattern. If local congregations are willing to be culturally flexible and not set one tradition in stone or sentimentalize a nostalgic, historical way of doing things, churches can exhibit more of the gospel's power to unite people across cultural barriers.

---

[18] Richard Bauckham, *Bible and Mission: Christian Mission in a Postmodern World* (Grand Rapids, MI: Baker, 2003), 9.

*Not every community is multi-ethnic, and so not
every church can or should be multi-ethnic. But, in
general, it is both theologically warranted (EPHESIANS
2) and missionally effective in our culture for North
American churches to be as multi-ethnic as possible
and to learn from and be connected to the multi-racial
global church.*

Creating a church committed to the poor and to justice[19]

It is important for churches to get the relationship
between words and deeds (evangelism and justice) right.
Justice must not replace evangelism, but on the other
hand, it must not be simply a means to the end of evangelism. We are to love our neighbors, sacrificially doing
good for them regardless of their beliefs. Pursuing justice,
then, is not to be ignored. And in order for churches to
follow a biblical understanding of justice, it is important
to know what biblical justice is *not*. Getting a grasp of
the reductionist theories of justice that can infect the
church (Marxism, Kantian individualism, utilitarianism)

---

[19] See *Generous Justice: How God's Grace Makes Us Just* (Penguin Books, 2016).

is crucial to keeping the church from straying from the gospel.

The biblical understanding of justice is unique in the way it espouses equal dignity and fairness; a special, practical respect and concern for the powerless; and radical generosity with money and possessions. The gospel's view on stewarding wealth, the causes of poverty, and our motivation to pursue justice uniquely distinguishes itself from today's views. When we make this distinction, we both prioritize the gospel and acknowledge the importance of justice.

Being a pioneer in civility, peace-making, and bridge-building

Ethnicity and economics are not the only ways Western culture is divided. We are also divided ideologically, and our public discourse discourages measured and generous exchange of ideas. In this context, Christians have an opportunity to model civility in a generation that desperately needs it. This involves practicing forgiveness and reconciliation both internally and externally. It means knowing the role of individual Christians in politics—avoiding both the illusion of pietism and the error of partisanship. It is taking care that the local church does not bind people's consciences where the Bible has left them free by making pronouncements on political matters that are matters not of biblical mandate but of prudential wisdom.[20] It is embodying these specific traits and methods when in dialogue with people who hold deeply different views:

- **Civility involves humility.** Humility includes recognizing the limits of what you can prove, understanding that everyone's position is based on unprovable faith assumptions about humanity and reality in some way, and critiquing others only on the basis of their own beliefs and framework, not yours.

- **Civility involves patience.** Patience requires giving sustained time to listening, understanding, and empathizing; identifying two things—the different experiences that divide us and the common experiences and commitments that unite us; and rooting this patience in Christian hope, avoiding both liberal utopianism and conservative nostalgia for the past.

---

[20] "Westminster Confession of Faith," Chapter 20, *Administrative Committee PCA*. Accessed August 21, 2019. https://www.pcaac.org/wp-content/uploads/2012/11/WCFScriptureProofs.pdf

- **Civility involves tolerance.** Tolerance shows respect for someone made in the image of God, even when the person is espousing something morally reprehensible. It does not require accepting views and behavior that are terribly wrong, nor refraining from calling out such things clearly.

- **Civility involves a lack of self-righteousness.** The gospel reminds us that we live unjustly, and so the gospel keeps us from despising and abusing oppressors. It keeps us from becoming oppressors ourselves as we seek to oppose oppression.

Having a church that is strongly pro-life

The doctrine of the image of God makes abortion a sin. Efforts to justify abortion of the unborn using arguments of capacity (no ability to make choices) end up justifying infanticide and killing elderly people with dementia. The early church's pro-life stance, however, was radically practical and not just political. It was committed to the whole lives of unwanted infants. Many made sacrifices not just to save their lives, but to support them with love and family throughout their entire lives. Today's church must not abstract a political pro-life stance—voting and supporting pro-life political candidates—from the sacrificial, practical support of children, women, long-term singles, and families. This cannot happen short of turning the church itself into a true family (1 Timothy 5). Creating the church as a true family is also central to the final element.

Becoming a sexual counter-culture

One of the greatest objections to Christianity today is that it has an outmoded sexual ethic. Many believe Christianity has an unhealthy, negative view of sexuality in general and of gay people in particular. The Christian view of sex is especially repugnant to today's understanding of self and identity. That view asserts the self's freedom to pursue fulfillment, and it also idealizes sexual expression and intimacy as a unique way to become an authentic self. The Christian sexual code is therefore considered both unrealistic and oppressive.

But we need to remember that the early church did not hold just one more of the many ancient, superstitious, taboo-laden cultural views of sexuality. The Christian sex ethic was revolutionary. It introduced the very idea of consent in sex, and it made sex *not* about self-fulfillment (which always privileges those with more power) but about creating lasting community that reflects God's relationship to us.[21] This is a higher, not lower, view of sex. The church also needs to argue that modern culture's sexual logic—that sex is for self-fulfillment and self-realization—ultimately depersonalizes and objectifies because it ultimately turns sex into a consumer good rather than as a means to nurture a bond of covenant. It leads to fractured community and the decline of marriage and the family. Sex outside of marriage is ultimately transactional and so it cannot finally be intimate. Culture's approach to sex, both in the Roman world and the modern world, has been bad for women (see #MeToo for proof). The Christian view requires sex to always be *super*-consensual—only for people ready to give their whole lives to each other. The church needs to create a sexual counterculture in its lived community, becoming a place where:

- Men and women refrain from sex before marriage;

- Men and women seek a marriage partner not on the basis of looks and wealth, but character;

- The unmarried—whether divorced, widowed, or never married—are incorporated as extended family members, having close friendships of both sexes and nurturing relationships with children;

---

[21] See Kyle Harper, *From Shame to Sin: The Christian Transformation of Sexual Morality in Late Antiquity* (Harvard University Press, 2016).

- People with same-sex attraction are valued members and are given support for their calling to chastity; and
- People who have struggled with issues of sex and gender are welcomed and listened to with humility, patience, and love.

COUNTER-CATECHESIS FOR A DIGITAL AGE

In the Sermon on the Mount, Jesus said, "You heard it said" before he said, "I say unto you" (Matthew 5:21-48). He did this not only to teach the truth, but also to do so in contrast to what the authorities of the day were saying. Our instruction needs to follow the same pattern. We need catechesis as well as *counter*-catechesis, using biblical doctrine to both deconstruct the beliefs of culture and answer questions of the human heart that culture's narratives cannot.

By using the word "catechesis," I am not necessarily calling for the use of the actual catechism method of question-and-answer (I am a proponent of that method, but that's not my point here). I use it to refer to the way churches have instructed and formed Christians who are shaped by the Bible and Christian teaching rather than by the world. The fact is that we have virtually stopped doing catechesis as it was done in the past. As a result, we have forgotten three things about formation.

Catechesis was always counter-catechesis.[22]

During the Reformation, there was an explosion of catechesis—new catechisms were written by the hundreds. It is worth noting that the Protestant catechisms gave less space to the doctrine of the Trinity or of Christ, and far more to the doctrine of salvation (justification and regeneration), to the sacraments, and to the church. This was because they were not merely incorporating their members into their teaching. They were also inoculating their members against the only real alternative to being a

We need a counter-catechism that explains, refutes, and re-narrates the world's catechisms to Christians.

Protestant: being a Catholic. The Protestant catechisms presented biblical doctrine against the Catholic catechisms, which also made them effective counter-catechisms. They not only constructed a world-view, but dismantled and vaccinated against the dominant alternatives.

The problem is that, as indispensable as the best of the catechisms are still (Heidelberg, Westminster, and Luther's Short and Large), they are insufficient. The main alter-

---

[22] I borrow this term from Alan Jacobs: "Dare to Make a Daniel," *Snakes and Ladders*. September 19, 2018. Accessed August 21, 2019. https://blog.ayjay.org/dare-to-make-a-daniel

native to being a Protestant Christian is now some form of Western secularism. The secular age has a very definite catechism of its own, and while our current instructional modes and catechisms may be biblically accurate, they do not present the truth in a way that clearly dismantles secular narratives and undermines secular beliefs.

Secular narratives are beliefs about reality that most cultural institutions inculcate as inarguable, obvious truths. They come to us now dozens of times a day—or even an hour—in ads, tweets, music, stories, opinion pieces, etc. They are narratives about:

- **Identity:** "You have to be true to yourself."

- **Freedom:** "You should be free to live as you choose, as long as you don't hurt anyone."

- **Happiness:** "You must do what makes you happiest. You can't sacrifice that for anyone."

- **Science:** "The only way to solve our problems is through objective science and facts."

- **Morality:** "Everyone has the right to decide what is right and wrong themselves."

- **Justice:** "We are obligated to work for the freedom, rights, and good of everyone in the world."

- **History:** "History is bending toward social progress and away from religion."

While each of these cultural messages is partly true (and indeed, despite distortions, rooted historically in Christian teaching), they are all theologically mistaken and pragmatically harmful to human life. Many biblical teachings and truths undermine, weaken, or balance out all of these narratives, and yet our current instruction does not show this. We need a counter-catechism that explains, refutes, and re-narrates the world's catechisms to Christians.

In our counter-catechesis, each of the basic narratives of the secular catechism will have to be identified, stated with examples from today's culture, affirmed in part because it usually represents a distortion or idolatrous imbalance of something true, subverted and critiqued, and shown to be fulfilled in its best form only in Christ.[23]

Catechesis was part of a moral ecology

In *The Content of Their Character*, James Davison Hunter and Ryan S. Olson explain that character can

---

[23] See Chapter 5, "Preaching and the Late Modern Mind" in Preaching: *Communicating Faith in an Age of Skepticism* (Penguin Books, 2016) for examples of how we can deconstruct the major cultural narratives today and engage them with the gospel.

never be imparted in a classroom, but only in a particular kind of community. Martin Luther King, Jr. is an example of this principle. He is often lifted up as an example of courage and commitment to justice, but an MLK, Jr. could not be produced by a classroom and textbooks alone. He was produced by the African-American church. Hunter and Olson call the kind of community that forges character a "moral ecology."[24] This is a community with the following elements.

A moral ecology first answers the question "*Why* be good?" The answer cannot simply be "because we say so." A strong moral ecology requires an account of the cosmos that grounds moral standards. The Bible does this, grounding its moral norms in the character of God and in a created human nature ordered toward certain goods—worship of the true God, the importance of work and family, and the sacrificial love of one's neighbor.

Second, a moral ecology answers the questions, "*What* specifically is good?" What is right worship, true love of neighbor, good work, and so on? Here again we have the moral instruction of the Bible, particularly the Ten Commandments, the book of Proverbs, the Sermon on the Mount, 1 Corinthians 13, as well as centuries of moral and ethical reflection on these texts.

---

[24] James Davison Hunter and Ryan S. Olson, *The Content of Their Character: Inquiries Into the Varieties of Moral Formation* (Finstock & Tew, 2017).

Third, a moral ecology answers the question "What is *not* good?" by contrasting biblical teaching with the moral values and discourse (or lack of them) in the culture. We must call out the practices and habits of heart within our society that lead not to human thriving but to personal and social deterioration.

Fourth, a moral ecology involves imagination (answering the question, "*Who* is good?"). It is not enough to merely give abstract principles. Our hearts are captured more by stories than by abstractions. All moral ecologies must provide actual, compelling embodiments of the moral principles. There have always been two kinds:

- Heroes and examples of the past. These exemplars can (and should) be both fictional and historical. It is important for writers, artists, filmmakers, and others to tell stories that point to the realities of good and evil.

- Contemporary models in one's own community. A moral ecology must have actual persons in the community to embody the standards in an attractive way.

Finally, a moral ecology involves *moral discourse* (answering the question, "*How* can we be good in daily life?"). Moral discourse is a dialogue of people asking, "How does the principle apply to this situation? What is the right thing to do here?"

Why is a moral ecology so crucial? The crisis is this: despite its incoherent moral cosmology, secular culture has created an enormously powerful, constantly immersive moral ecology through the digital revolution that overwhelms the two or three hours a week Christians worship and study in church.

The amount of time we spend on our phones in a day—the number of images and videos and repetitive slogans we see—makes the most immersive set of practices ever. It engages the imagination with narratives. It makes the influence and consumption of TV (already a concern a generation ago) look tiny by comparison. Those consuming digital content are being deeply catechized for far more hours in a week and far more effectively than anything the church is doing. It would not be going too far to call it brainwashing of the purportedly benign type seen in George Orwell's *1984*.

It is no surprise that so many young people raised in the church, taught and instructed for years, say, "I don't see what's wrong about two people having sex if they really love each other." Alarmed parents can point them to biblical texts, but they won't be effective because the underlying narratives that make such a view of sex plausible—narratives of identity and freedom and morality—were never identified as such and exposed as implausible. We have to learn to form Christians who are shaped more by the biblical narrative than by cultural narratives.

James K. A. Smith has helped us see that character formation flows as much from the engagement of the imagination (through liturgical worship, art, and story) as it does from intellectual instruction.[25] Our work of counter-catechesis should therefore include the following:

- New tools of catechesis that are formed to present the basics of Christian truth as a direct contrast to the narratives of late modern culture (e.g., "You have heard it said—but I say unto you")

- Worship that combines ancient patterns of liturgy with culturally contextualized forms

- Use of the arts to convey the Christian story

- Theological training of both ministers and lay leaders that equips them to carry out these kinds of formative practices

---

[25] James. K. A. Smith, *Imagining the Kingdom: How Worship Works* (Cultural Liturgies, Book 2) (Baker Academic, 2013).

- A rediscovery of rich devotional practices that are nearly extinct because of the busyness of our schedules

This process of formation is part of the *inward move* of a missionary encounter. Done well, this formation will equip Christians to make an *outward move* into their workplaces and other spheres of influence.

FAITHFUL CHRISTIAN PRESENCE IN PUBLIC SPHERES

For years, the churches in the West assumed that their members lived in a culture that was the product of Christianity. Lesslie Newbigin points out that when Christians worked in the fields of education, medicine, art, music, agriculture, politics, and economics, they did not need to ask the church for guidance. In general, the acknowledged masters in each field would operate on the basis of fundamentally Christian understandings of reality and morality. That meant that the churches could:

without immediate and obvious disaster, confine themselves to specifically 'religious' concerns, to the provision for opportunities for worship, religious teaching, and fellowship, knowing that their members will, in their secular occupations, still have some real possibility of maintaining Christian standards of thought and practice. Thus, the Churches [tended] to become loosely compacted fellowships within a wider semi-Christian culture…[26]

This, of course, has all changed. Now, we live in a culture dominated by non-Christian thought and themes (about reason/science, individualism, relativism, materialism). Even though non-Christian culture may contain a vast amount of good, believers are members of a community animated by a set of sharply different principles. And this reality requires us to decide how to faithfully engage the world around us.

James Hunter, professor of Religion, Culture, and Social Theory at the University of Virginia, identifies three cultural strategies Christians have tried over the years—all of them flawed—in his book *To Change the World: The Irony, Tragedy, and Possibility of Christianity in the Late Modern World*:

- Be defensive against culture and seek to dominate it,

- Seek purity from culture and withdraw from it entirely,

---

[26] Lesslie Newbigin, *Lesslie Newbigin: Missionary Theologian: A Reader* (Eerdmans, 2006), 118.

• Compromise with culture and be assimilated by it.

As an alternative to these, Hunter argues what we should strive for instead is faithful presence within the culture. According to Hunter, Christians do not withdraw from culture, but they do not compromise and they do not try to dominate. They simply enter every field trying to be salt and light, trying to serve, and yet at the same time being true to their Christian faith. They're *faithful*, which means they stay true to the Bible, but they're *present*.

Pursuing "faithful presence" today will be controversial. Elizabeth Bruenig, who writes on religion for the *Washington Post*, wrote a fascinating article called "In God's Country" about how evangelicals' view of changing culture has shifted over time.[27] Using different terms, she suggests essentially that the primary evangelical strategy of the previous generation was defensive against culture, to work to change society by taking power and legislating Christian laws. Today, by contrast, evangelicals don't expect to change society. They feel like that ship has sailed. Today, they want to protect their lifestyle in a bubble so they can live the way they want to live. The impulse to

---

[27] Elizabeth Bruenig, "In God's Country: Evangelicals View Trump as Their Protector. Will They Stand by Him in 2020?" *The Washington Post*, August 14, 2019. https://www.washingtonpost.com/opinions/2019/08/14/evangelicals-view-trump-their-protector-will-they-stand-by-him

shape society is replaced by the impulse to retreat from it.

In other words, faithful presence may run counter to the primary way evangelicals presently engage culture. That means every Christian will need guidance from fellow Christians, and not merely about private spiritual disciplines and in religious gatherings. Rather, believers will need help from the church for thinking and living at every decisive point, in public as well as private life, in life within the workplace as well as within the church.

Every society has a "cultural economy," a set of public sectors in which ideas and practices are forged that will direct how people live in the culture. These include the academy, business, the arts, the media, law and government, and many others. This means that the church must train and disciple Christians to integrate their faith with their work in these public spheres, "in the daily business of…the councils of government, the board rooms of trans-national corporations, the trade unions, the universities, and the schools." [28] This is an expansive vision for Christian influence in every area of human life, not because Christians are dominant there, but because they are faithful there. For this vision to be realized, Newbigin argues,

---

[28] Lesslie Newbigin, "Can the West Be Converted?" (St Colm's Education Centre and College, 1984).

We need to create, above all, possibilities in every congregation for laypeople to seek illumination from the gospel for their daily secular duty... The work of scientists, economists, political philosophers, artists and others [must be] illuminated by insights derived from rigorous theological thinking. For such a declericalized theology, the role of the church will be that of servant, not mistress.[29]

This last statement, that the church is a "servant," is crucial. Within Christendom, it is the clergy who have "all the answers" for how to do mission. But pastors do not know enough about every vocational field to know how the gospel influences work in that sector. In this endeavor, clergy and laypeople sit down as equals—each with some knowledge the other does not have—to plan for Christian witness in public life.

Christians are often told to keep their values and faith out of the public sphere, otherwise they will be imposing their views on others. Of course, this makes the false assumption that it is possible to do one's work without reference to comprehensive beliefs derived from a coherent worldview. And, ironically, to tell individuals

---

[29] Lesslie Newbigin, *Foolishness to the Greeks: The Gospel and Western Culture* (Eerdmans, 1988).

they must keep their beliefs private is to impose secular beliefs about religion and the world on Christians. Instead, the church should train Christians not to seal off their faith from their work, but to think out the implications of their Christian beliefs from their work.

Matthew 5:13 tells us that we are to be "salt of the earth." This is a wonderful metaphor. In ancient times, salt was used not only to bring flavor out of meat, but also to preserve it from decay. So when Jesus said we are the salt of the earth, he meant we're supposed to be honest, work hard, do good, and keep things from becoming corrupt—but also be open about our Christianity. Jeremiah 29 tells us that after the Israelites were exiled to Babylon, they were to seek the peace of the city—plant gardens, build houses, and seek its prosperity. We can still serve people, be good neighbors, and be involved in culture while being faithful to and open about our Christianity.

If Christians are equipped to do this, the gospel will become "salt and light" in culture more naturally than if we took a more political approach in which Christians sought to gain the reins of coercive power, or took a more withdrawn approach in which being a Christian was seen as something you did only in private with no application to every area of life.

GRACE TO THE POINT

We must never lose grasp of the difference between gospel grace and religious moralism. Why does the Protestant church constantly fall into the temptation to self-righteousness, dominance, and exclusion? Why does it fail to reproduce the early church's social mandate? Because it loses its grip on the very core of its faith.

Through the last few centuries, the church in various parts of the world has experienced times of renewal called awakenings or revivals. During these seasons, the church is marked by strong growth through conversions, by genuine cultural engagement leading to positive social changes, and by both the planting of new churches and the renewal of older congregations. What leads to such times? There are many features of these movements, but at the heart of them all is a rediscovery of the gospel of grace—totally free to us, yet infinitely costly to our Savior.[30]

When we lapse back into thinking that we are saved by our moral efforts, we become enmeshed in both pride and fear—pride because we may think God and the world owe us acclaim; fear because we can never be sure

---

[30] See Richard Lovelace, *Dynamics of Spiritual Life: An Evangelical Theology of Renewal*, IVP Academic, 1979.

we've lived truly good-enough lives. And so, when we lose the existential (or the doctrinal) grasp on the truth that we are saved by faith alone through grace alone because of Christ alone, we not only lose our joy and fall into fear, but we also lose our graciousness and fall into pride. The world, of course, is quick—too quick—to find fault with the church and thus justify its dismissal of the gospel message. And yet it is quite right to do so. If the church continually moves toward dominance and control rather than love and service, it shows that it doesn't really believe the gospel it preaches. If the church doesn't believe the gospel, why should the world?

In *Shantung Compound*, Langdon Gilkey's experience in a Japanese internment camp showed him that many religious people were just as selfish and exploitative as irreligious people. Though many missionaries had been taken hostage, they started to form cliques and looked out only for themselves. Yet Gilkey saw something quite different in Eric Liddell. Liddell (the Olympic Gold Medalist of *Chariots of Fire* fame) didn't just worry about his own self. He spent tireless hours caring for elderly prisoners, teaching classes on the Bible and science, and organizing games and dances for the children, right until the day of his death. This sacrifice brought Gilkey to see the difference between generic moralism and a religion of grace. He concluded:

Religion is not the place where the problem of man's egotism is automatically solved. Rather, it is there that the ultimate battle between human pride and God's grace takes place. Insofar as human pride may win the battle, religion can and does become one of the instruments of human sin. But insofar as there the self does meet God and so can surrender to something beyond its own self-interest, religion may provide the one possibility for a much needed and very rare release from our common self-concern.[31]

Yes—rare! But the gospel brings this release. There is no hope without it.

---

[31] Langdon Gilkey, *Shantung Compound: The Story of Men and Women Under Pressure* (Harper & Row, 1966), 193.

ENCOURAGEMENTS

The challenges and responsibilities outlined here are formidable. It would be easy to be discouraged. We have, at least, these encouragements:

THE RISE OF GLOBAL CHRISTIANITY

While the situation may look bleak for Christianity in the West, the West is no longer the center for Christianity. One of the main developments of the 20th and 21st centuries is the explosive growth of non-Western Christianity, the vast majority of which is evangelical/Pentecostal. At the very least, 70% of all Christians today live outside of the West, and many believers in Western countries are non-Anglo people from non-Western countries. There are more Presbyterians in Ghana than in the U.S. and the U.K. There are more Anglicans in Nigeria alone than in all of the U.S. and the U.K. The reality is that the most secular populations of North America and Europe are in decline. Meanwhile, through evangelism and birth-rate, Christianity is growing rapidly, and through immigration and mission work the church will continue to thrive and grow in many places in the West. As a result, the number of all people who are "secular" or who have "no religious preference" is expected to decline from 16% to 13% by mid-century.[32]

THE POWER OF *CHOSEN* RELIGION

If late modern culture rejects most aspects of evangelical Christianity, there is one feature of it, at least, that Western people find appealing: its emphasis on choice. Some religions can be largely *inherited* in form. There are religions you are born into and adhere to because of family background or nationality. "Of course I'm Lutheran. I'm Norwegian," or "I'm Catholic because I'm Italian," or "I'm Hindu because I'm Indian." Today, however, the emphasis is on individual choice and decision. Young people do not want to follow a path that they have not chosen for themselves. This is why traditionally inherited religion—Catholicism and mainline Protestantism—is in sharp decline. In Europe, the state churches are emptying. Evangelical faith is far better suited to such a cultural situation because it insists on a personal decision of faith and a conversion experience for everyone. Nevertheless, evangelical faith, while well-adapted to the culture of individual choice, also appropriately challenges it. When

---

[32] "Why People with No Religion Are Projected to Decline as a Share of the World's Population" Pew Research Center, April 7, 2017. https://www.pewresearch.org/fact-tank/2017/04/07/why-people-with-no-religion-are-projected-to-decline-as-a-share-of-the-worlds-population

we freely choose to follow Christ, we also choose to give up living according to our own lights and submit to his loving authority.

THE CULTURE-FORMATIVE POWER OF CITIES

Much of the energy of Christian growth today is among non-white, non-Western people and young people who want chosen religion, not inherited religion. This is why the great cities of the West may become hotbeds of new, growing churches. There, the populations are both young and multi-ethnic. Cities are the culture-forming wombs of modern society. Through agglomeration—the amassing of talent in urban proximity—new innovations and creative enterprises arise and spread out to the rest of the culture. If churches thrive and grow in cities, and if increasing numbers of urban Christians demonstrate their commitment to mercy and justice and integrate their faith with their work in business, the arts, the media, and the academy, then Christians will continue to be salt and light in society.

EVERYTHING IS UNPRECEDENTED ONCE

Up until 1900, there had never been a fast-growing revival in a non-Western pre-Christian country. Then there was the Korean Presbyterian revival in 1907 and the East African Anglican revival in the 1930s. There was never a renewal movement of monasticism until there was. There was never a Reformation until there was. There never was anything like a Great Awakening until there was.

There has never been a fast-growing revival in a post-Christian, secular society. But every great new thing is unprecedented—until it happens. Jesus said, "I will build my church, and the gates of hell will not prevail against it" (Matthew. 16:18). There's no reason to believe this promise has an expiration date.

WHAT WE NEED NOW: COLLABORATIVE INDEPENDENCE

What will it take to move the church toward a missionary encounter with Western culture? The answer is collaborative yet independent thinking.

Why collaboration? There simply is no one denomination or tradition that is historically strong in all of these areas—evangelism and formation, high theory yet revival and spiritual awakening, mercy and justice *and* faith and work integration *and* historic Christian sexual ethics. Who is sufficient for these things? No one of us, or no one church.

Why independent thinking? As Lesslie Newbigin noted repeatedly, the Western church has been made captive to the 'gods' of secular culture, but different branches of people pursue different idols. As a result, every part of the agenda above will attract anger or opposition from one part of the church. Evangelism and sexual ethics will arouse the hostility of the mainline church; emphasis on racial and economic justice will alarm many in the evangelical churches. Those working toward a missionary encounter will need to listen to their critics as a good discipline of self-examination, but in the end, they cannot follow them into their respective cultural captivities.